NATIONAL CAREER DEVELOPMENT ASSOCIATION

CAREER KNOWLEDGE SERIES

DESIGNING AND IMPLEMENTING
CAREER SERVICES

National Career Development Association
A founding division of the American Counseling Association

NCDA opposes discrimination against any individual based on age, culture, disability, ethnicity, race, religion/spirituality, creed, gender, gender identity and expression, sexual orientation, marital/partnership status, language preference, socioeconomic status, or any other personal characteristic not specifically relevant to job performance.

(Approved by the NCDA Board - October 2013)

Printed in the United States of America.

© Copyright 2015 by the National Career Development Association
305 North Beech Circle
Broken Arrow, OK 74012
Phone: (918) 663-7060
Fax: (918) 663-7058
www.ncda.org

Library of Congress Cataloging-in-Publication Data

Designing and implementing career services / National Career Development Association.
        volumes ; cm
Contents: The importance of planning -- The steps of the program development process -- Supportive roles -- Summary -- Reference -- Resources -- Online web resources.
ISBN 978-1-885333-46-9
1. Vocational guidance--Information services. 2. Career development--Vocational guidance. I. National Career Development Association (U.S.)
HF5381.D4532 2015
362'.0425--dc23
2014033916

Introduction

The National Career Development Association (NCDA) inspires and empowers the achievement of career and life goals by providing professional development, resources, standards, scientific research, and advocacy. NCDA is a founding division of the American Counseling Association (ACA).

NCDA is the recognized leader in developing standards for the career development profession, for the provision of career programs and services, and for the evaluation of career information materials. NCDA works with licensing and credentialing bodies to support the preparation and recognition of career professionals. NCDA also sets ethical standards for the career development profession including guidelines for the provision of career services on the Internet.

NCDA's Career Knowledge Series is designed for individuals wishing to understand career development. Titles in this series include:

- Providing Career Services to Multicultural Populations

- The Role of Career Information and Technological Resources in Career Planning

- Job Seeking and Employability Skills

- Designing and Implementing Career Services

- Developing a Helping Relationship

- Training and Leading Groups

- Career Development Theory and Its Application

- The Role of Assessment in Career Planning

Each title provides a thorough introduction and discussion for its specialized topic.

NOTE ABOUT TERMS USED: Though the person who receives career services may be referred to as a student or participant in different settings, we will use the word client throughout this unit and the entire Career Knowledge Series to refer to that person. Individuals providing career services may work in a number of fields and have a variety of titles or designations. We will use the general terms of provider, career services provider, career practitioner, or career professional to refer to individuals delivering career services to clients.

NATIONAL CAREER DEVELOPMENT ASSOCIATION

CAREER KNOWLEDGE SERIES

DESIGNING AND IMPLEMENTING CAREER SERVICES

This topic provides resources for planning and delivering career services to different populations. Specifically, the topic describes 12 steps for planning and implementation. Strategically planning career services is critical with limited human and fiscal resources that organizations face, and this topic provides concrete ideas and suggestions for delivering career services.

Table of Contents

Designing and Implementing Career Services

The purpose of this unit is to give you the knowledge, skills, and confidence that you need to plan and deliver the services needed by different populations that you serve. The unit will describe 12 specific steps of planning and implementation. In completing the unit, you will have an opportunity to practice these steps by planning some program of services for a population that you currently work with or may work with in the future. When you complete these activities, you will have valuable tools to apply in your work setting. As you read this unit, imagine different populations that you might focus on in this activity and some of the ways in which you might meet their needs.

The Importance of Planning

For at least three significant reasons, it is important to plan and design programs and services, rather than to deal with each client's needs as totally unique.

- First, your clients have common needs (for example, learning to manage a successful job search) as well as unique needs (such as referral to a specific agency). Time and money can be saved by addressing common needs with a single program of services delivered in small groups or by technology. This makes it possible to serve more clients with the resources that you have on hand. This can be especially important when time and budgets are limited.

- Second, services can be much more effective when they are developed through the process described in this unit. Since this process requires you to identify specific needs and to detail objectives and possible ways to accomplish them, it requires you to invest careful thought in the design.

- Third, today's organizations demand accountability, which is an important key to sustainability. Well-designed programs provide both the basis for measuring accomplishments (i.e., measurable objectives) and the plan (i.e., evaluation) for doing so. For that reason, thoughtfully designed programs are more likely to be successful and last longer.

ACTIVITY #1: THINK ABOUT PLANNING

Think about the amount of planning that goes into the services or products that are provided by your present or a past employer. Identify the positive outcomes when planning is done well and the negative outcomes when planning is not done well.

The Steps of the Program Development Process

Developing cost-effective programs of services is both an art and a science. The purpose of such development is to plan detailed services to meet client needs. It is likely that you will be tasked with this responsibility or that you will serve as a member of a team that works through the planning process together. So, as you read this unit, think carefully about the practical application of each of these steps in the site where you work or in one in which you would like to work.

Step 1. Scan the environment.

All career services are delivered within the context of a specific environment. The environments in which you may design and deliver programs may be as varied as schools, human resources offices of organizations, OneStop centers, prisons, military transition centers, or AARP centers for older adults. The environment will have a profound effect upon the content, funding, delivery, and evaluation of your program. So, as a first step, it is important that you identify the characteristics of that environment that you must consider in the planning of your program. In that process, you will need to think about the answers to these questions:

- What are the current priorities of the administration?

- To what extent does management support your goals for the organization?

- What factors in the environment may impact what you can deliver and how you can deliver it?

- What organizational time constraints may impact service delivery?

- What kinds of restraints or guidelines are provided by internal (such as budget or type of organization) or external (such as the goals of the funding source or legislation) sources?

The answers to these and other relevant questions will provide a framework into which your program must fit comfortably in order to be successful.

Step 2. Define and describe the target population.

The purpose of this step is to get a clear picture of the individuals who will receive your services. It is not possible to design effective programs without this knowledge. The characteristics of persons who receive your services may be mandated by the legislation that provides your funding (such as programs for adults who need to be re-skilled, welfare-to-work programs, or programs for older adults) or may be partially determined by the setting (such as a OneStop center, a college or university, or a military transition center) in which you work. In other kinds of settings, such as a community center, there may be a wider range of characteristics. Regardless of the setting, it is important to find answers to the following questions:

- What is the age range of the targeted population?
- What is the percentage of individuals within subgroups of that total age range?
- What is the proportion of males and females?
- What multicultural populations are represented within the group? What is the distribution by levels of education?
- For what percentage is English a second language?
- What is the geographic distribution of those who might use the program?
- What percent of the population is currently employed? Unemployed?
- What distinctive characteristics, if any, does the population have?
- What reasons do clients have for coming to your site for career planning services?

If you develop a program in a site that has been in operation for a year or more, it may be possible to acquire much of this information from past records. If the site is new or if no data have been collected in the past, you will need to collect the data by administering a questionnaire (a sample is included as Figure 1.1) or via intake interviews. In either case, it is important to collect the same information from all participants.

This information should then be entered into a database from which summary reports can be provided as well as lists of individuals who fit certain combinations of characteristics (for example, single mothers under 25 years of age or unemployed adults over 50).

Knowing the characteristics of your clients will help you with program design in the following ways:

- You will be able to design programs that are unique to subgroups of the total population.
- You will be able to identify members of those subgroups to participate in the programs you design.
- You will be able to deliver some or all parts of the program to two or more persons at the same time.

You may be the person who analyzes the records of clients for the past two to three years in order to summarize their characteristics. You may also be the person who customizes the questionnaire, word-processes and duplicates it, or uploads it to the Internet using an automated survey tool (such as Survey Monkey). Or, you may incorporate these questions into your intake interviews and summarize the data for your supervisor. The summary might look something like the one included as Figure 1.2.

Step 3. Identify and describe the needs of the target population.

The purpose of this step is to understand the specific needs of the entire target population and/or of subgroups within it so that you can plan the content of the services you will provide. Sometimes the needs of a given target population are *predefined*. This means that they may be determined by a set of guidelines. For example, the *National Career Development Guidelines* (see Online Web Resources for the web address) identify career competencies that individuals should acquire at specific ages. Similarly, some states, counties, and local districts have developed their own guidelines. The Workforce Investment Act (WIA) specifies how funds can be used for employment and training of adult and dislocated workers.

Sometimes a program of services becomes possible because of funding gained through the competitive proposal-writing process. In such cases, the objectives of the program are clearly defined by the funding source, and the program must be designed to meet those objectives.

In situations in which needs are not predefined, there are four ways in which they can be identified: questionnaires, structured intake interviews, focus groups, and expert judgment. Ideally, two or more of these methods would be used.

- In the *questionnaire* approach, some or all members of the proposed target population are asked to respond in writing to questions aimed at assessing their needs.

- In the *structured interview* approach, selected members of the proposed target population are all asked the same questions, but respond verbally. The questions or items used in a questionnaire or in a structured interview should be essentially the same. The difference is in the way in which the questionnaire is administered: as a form that each incoming client completes (such as that included as Figure 1.1) or as a part of a structured interview during which the interviewer completes a worksheet.

- *Focus groups* are made up of 6–12 people who represent the total target population or identified subgroups within it. They may be asked to give 60–90 minutes of their time to meet as a group led by you or by someone on your development team. Here are some useful guidelines for forming focus groups:

  - They should be representative of the target population. In other words, if 70% of the members of the target group are female, the composition of the group should roughly mirror this. If 35% are between the ages of 40 and 50, the group should approximately mirror this fact. Obviously, with small groups it will not be possible to mirror all characteristics, so some predominant ones—gender, age, ethnicity, employment status—might be used.

  - Individuals should serve voluntarily, by invitation.

  - Individuals should receive a thorough description, preferably in writing, of the topics that will be discussed in the focus group. They should know that the reason for their participation is to develop services that will be beneficial to them.

- In the *expert judgment* approach, one or more persons who are considered to be experts in both the target population and career development are asked to identify the population's predominant needs, based on research and experience with the population. The judgment of these persons is then used as the basis for developing the objectives and content of the program of services.

FIGURE 1.1
Sample Client Intake Form (OneStop Center)
Please complete all parts of this questionnaire. Its content will be used to provide services that will meet your needs.

Name:_____

Marital status: ☐ Married   ☐ Single   ☐ Divorced/separated

Address:_____

Home phone: _____/_____ E-mail: _____

City/State/Zip: _____ Work phone: _____/_____

Gender: ☐ M   ☐ F

Education (check all that apply):   *Age range:*   *Racial-ethnic membership:*
☐ Didn't complete high school   ☐ 16-20   ☐ African American
☐ Graduated from high school   ☐ 21–25   ☐ Asian
☐ Completed vocational-technical   ☐ 26–30   ☐ Hispanic
   school or community college   ☐ 31–35   ☐ Native American
☐ Completed some college   ☐ 36–40   ☐ White
☐ Graduated from college   ☐ 41–45   ☐ Other:
☐ Graduate work   ☐ 46–50   ☐ Check if English is a
☐ Military service   ☐ 51–55   second language for you.
☐ Apprenticeship   ☐ over 55

Employment: Are you currently ☐ employed or ☐ unemployed? List past 3 jobs:

Type of job: Employer: Dates of employment:

_____   _____   _____

_____   _____   _____

_____   _____   _____

Reasons you came (check all that apply):
☐ Talk with someone about a job or
   job change
☐ Take some tests
☐ Use resources to learn about
   occupations or schools
☐ Get help with transportation
☐ Use a computer to write a resume
☐ Use the Internet to find a job
☐ Learn how to find job openings
☐ Learn to complete a job application
   or resume
☐ Learn how to have a job interview
☐ Other:_____

Services you want (check all that apply):
☐ Help with getting a job
☐ Help with changing jobs
☐ Get some training
☐ Get help with child care or eldercare
☐ Make some career goals
☐ Be referred to an agency for help
☐ Other:_____

FIGURE 1.2
Summary of Client Demographic Data and Needs

432 Number of clients included in this summary

Marital status: **61%** married   **19%** single   **20%** divorced or separated

Gender: **38%** male   **62%** female

Education:	*Age Range:*	*Racial-Ethnic Mix:*
23% Didn't complete high school	**12%** 16–20	**23%** African American
35% Graduated from high school	**8%** 21–25	**11%** Asian
8% Completed vo-tech or comm. coll.	**7%** 26–30	**25%** Hispanic
14% Completed some college	**15%** 31–35	**4%** Native American
16% Graduated from college	**17%** 36–40	**26%** White
4% Completed some graduate work	**18%** 41–45	**11%** Other
16% Served in military	**13%** 46–50	**34%** English as
7% Had apprenticeship training	**7%** 51–55	second language
	3% over 55	

Employment: **53%** unemployed **47%** employed

Reasons for coming:
24% Talk with someone to help with getting or changing a job
12% Take some tests
42% Use resources to learn about occupations or schools
21% Use a computer to write a resume
10% Make a career plan
21% Use the Internet to find a job
47% Learn how to find job openings
32% Learn to complete job application or resume
25% Learn how to have a job interview
12% Other: _____

Stated needs:
53% Get a job
20% Change from a present job
12% Get some training
15% Get some help with child care or eldercare
17% Get some help with transportation
21% Make some career goals
11% Get referral to an agency that can help
14% Other needs: _____

The leader of the focus group asks questions, encourages everyone to participate, reflects and summarizes the feedback provided, and, after participants have left, writes a brief summary of the suggestions and information gathered. Important questions to ask vary with setting and populations, but the following list may be adapted for most settings:

- What are the needs that you currently have related to your job or career?

- Which of these needs is the most urgent?

- How do you hope that this center (organization, program) can help you meet these needs?

- How much time each week can you devote to getting help?

- How would you prefer to receive assistance? (e.g., self-help print materials, telephone, e-mail, in-person discussion, group presentations, website)

- What barriers might affect your ability to receive or benefit from these services?

The answers to these questions can provide invaluable knowledge about the content of services, expectations of clients, time availability, ways to provide service, and barriers to success.

Information gained from questionnaires, intake interviews, and/or focus groups may be combined with expert knowledge to form a summary of client needs. A review of the literature of career development or insight provided by a consultant could reveal, for example, that many members of the target population have poor self-concepts, poor decision-making skills, and little faith in being able to control their own lives. Members of a focus group may not know this fact or be able to express this need clearly. For this reason, it is desirable to add expert judgment to data collected through other means. A summary of the data collected, as illustrated in Figure 1.2, will serve as an invaluable foundation for writing objectives, selecting and developing program content, and selecting methods of service delivery.

Step 4. Identify the stakeholders.

Stakeholders are persons or entities who have vested interest in and/or may be affected by the program or services that you plan to offer. They may either support and enhance your program or may place roadblocks in its way. They may be either *internal* or *external* to your organization. Those who are *internal* are employees or volunteers within your organization and probably have the same goals for clients as you do. *Externals* are individuals or organizations that are separate from yours, but have a similar mission or provide supportive services, and might collaborate with your team in funding, developing, or delivering the services.

Stakeholders have varying degrees of power to affect you, either positively or negatively. Though a first assumption may be that internal stakeholders have greater power than external stakeholders, this may not be the case. The following are some examples of stakeholders in different settings:

- In schools, colleges, and universities:
  - Students
  - Administrators
  - Parents
  - Employers
  - Instructors

- In Workforce Development centers (OneStop career centers):
  - Clients
  - Administrators
  - Employers
  - Co-workers not involved in program delivery

- In military transition centers:
  - Service personnel
  - Family of service personnel
  - Administrators
  - Employers
  - Legislators
  - Taxpayers

- In community non-profit organizations (such as Goodwill, Inc.):
  - Clients
  - Administrators
  - Volunteers
  - Employers

- In faith-based organizations:
  - Clients
  - Paid staff of the organization
  - Volunteers
  - Board members of the organization
  - Members of the organization
  - Employers
  - The general community

In marketing your program, described in Step 10, it is important to build a positive relationship with these stakeholders and to keep them informed and represented during the program design phase of the plan. Representatives of these groups might be included in focus groups or on the planning team that develops objectives, content, and modes of service delivery.

Step 5. Write clear, concrete, measurable objectives.

The reason for writing objectives is to force you to focus on what you are trying to accomplish in the program—what you want the outcomes to be for the participants. Objectives will become the guidelines for program development and evaluation. For that reason they need to be very clear and specific, and they also need to be measurable in ways that are realistic in the program site. Based on what you have learned about the needs of your clients, there may be one or several different programs or sequences of activities that are needed to meet them. Each of these different programs should have its own list of 3–6 measurable objectives. For example, we could conclude from the summary in Figure 1.2 that we should develop three programs (or sequences of activities) to meet common needs. Additional unique needs can be met through individual work with specific clients.

Program objectives should have the following characteristics:

- They should cover critical points of the content needed to meet identified needs.

- Each objective should state some outcome for the participants that can be realistically measured.

- When possible, the objectives should state under what condition(s) the outcome would be reached.

- They should be one sentence in length, starting with "By the end of this (program, course, workshop, activity) participants will be able to …."

The three programs identified to meet common needs for the sample population in Figure 1.1 could be the following:

1. How to decide what kind of job to enter

2. How to find job openings

3. How to prepare for a successful interview (including making the initial contact, completing job applications or writing a resume, and participating in a successful job interview)

The word *measurable* means that there is a reasonable way to find out whether the clients were able to achieve the objective. In university settings, it may be suitable to have an objective which says "At the end of the program, students will have increased their career maturity by 25% or more as measured by Super's *Career Development Inventory* (Super, 1988). It is reasonable in that setting because it may be possible to have two randomly selected or matched groups of clients, one which receives the program and one which does not, during the time of the evaluation of this objective. It may also be reasonable to purchase the Career Development Inventory and to have a graduate student administer it to the group that received the program and run a statistical analysis to compare the results of the two groups.

This objective would not be realistic or measurable in a OneStop center due to the fact that it would not be possible to select two comparable groups and then to deny service to one for a period of time. Staff time and expertise to administer this assessment and to perform statistical tests on its results might also be problematic. In that setting, the objective "At the end of this series of workshops, clients will be able to list three jobs that would allow them to transfer the skills they acquired through past work experience" would be realistic. It would also be measurable, since clients could be asked to list the three jobs they identified, either on a questionnaire administered at the end of a program or during an exit interview.

Some measurable objectives for the three different groups that might be drawn from the population described in Figure 1.1 are as follows:

For program 1. Decide what kind of job to enter

At the end of this sequence of activities, clients will be able to

1. State their interests as a description of a Holland code

2. List the transferable skills that they currently have

3. Give the titles of at least three occupations or jobs in which these interests and skills can be used, and describe these occupations or jobs related to daily work tasks, employment outlook, needed training, and beginning salary range

For program 2. Find job openings

At the end of this sequence of activities clients, will be able to

1. Demonstrate that they can use at least three methods to find job openings in the occupations that interest them

2. Name three companies that have the kind of jobs they want and describe the goods or services they produce

3. Describe jobs of interest in each of the companies, and

4. State how their skills can be related to the tasks of the available job(s)

For program 3. Prepare for a successful job interview

At the end of this sequence of activities, clients will be able to

1. Relate their own interests and skills to the jobs they are seeking

2. Prepare a job application or resume that highlights their particular skills for a specific job, and

3. Participate in a mock job interview in which they demonstrate good interview behavior and are able to link their skills and experience to the needs of the employer

Step 6. Determine how the program of services will be evaluated.

When you invest time and thought in the development of measurable objectives, program evaluation is relatively easy. The task in this step is to find out whether the people who have completed your program have accomplished the objectives you specified for them. One reason for evaluation is to determine the success of your program for your own satisfaction. A second reason is to be able to report the program results to management. If the results are positive, you may be able to conclude that clients have benefited enough to justify the expense of the program. Third, and also very important, data will be gathered which will be used to improve the program the next time it is offered. All three reasons should be kept in mind when evaluation is planned.

One well-known model for evaluation is that developed by Kirkpatrick (1994). It proposes that evaluation can be completed at four different levels, each deeper in meaning than the previous. The first level of this model, *reaction*, seeks feedback from the participants about such things as how they liked the instructor, methods of instruction, program publicity, etc. This feedback may be gathered through group discussion, individual exit interviews, or a web-based or print follow-up questionnaire.

The second level of the Kirkpatrick model, *learning*, determines how much knowledge the participants learned through the program. This level might be assessed by means of an end-of-program exam or via a pre-program and post-program assessment designed to measure how much change occurs in participants' scores due to the "treatment" (i.e., program of services provided). For example, concepts such as knowledge of the world of work, knowledge of good job-seeking skills, or knowledge of good decision-making skills might be assessed.

The third level of the Kirkpatrick model, *behavior*, is designed to measure changes in participants' behavior due to participation in the program. While in Level 2 the participants' knowledge of how to get a job might be measured, in Level 3 whether or not they actually did engage in a successful job search would be measured.

The fourth level of the model, *results*, is designed to answer the question "So, what difference did it make?" If dislocated workers, for example, acquired some new skills and were able to become employed after participating in the program, were they able to remain employed? Were they able to move from unemployed status to employed status and maintain that position? How much government funding was saved because they moved from needing support to being able to contribute to the tax base? What was the return on investment (ROI) for this program?

How services will be evaluated differs significantly in different settings, dependent both on what kind of evaluation is possible in a given setting and on what Kirkpatrick model level management expects. Evaluation may range from completion of a questionnaire in some sites to a very carefully designed and controlled study in other sites. Whatever the type of evaluation is, it must be focused on finding out whether people achieved the objectives that were set. Figure 1.3 provides examples of some ways to do the evaluation. The end product of this phase will be a summary of how well the objectives were met, including recommendations on how to improve the program the next time it is offered.

The evaluation that you plan will consist of some combination of the following methods:

- A questionnaire administered at the end of the program of services or an exit interview—The questionnaire administered in either way will ask direct questions designed to determine whether each objective was met. There may not be a one-to-one relationship. In other words, there may be multiple questions targeted at one objective or one question designed to measure the accomplishment of two or more objectives.

- A before-and-after objective test—In this method, the purpose is to note the difference in an individual's score or of the group's mean score before and after the program's delivery. Of course, the goal is that the "post" scores (after delivery of the program) be higher than the "pre" scores (those before delivery of the program).

- An observational test—In this method, some accomplishment covered in the objectives is observed by one or more persons who are qualified to judge its quality. For example, if an objective relates to being able to write a professional resume, its accomplishment can be measured by reviewing the resumes developed by individuals in the program. Similarly, if an objective related to the percent of participants who were able to find a job, it could be measured by a follow-up study that determined how many participants did, in fact, enter the job market.

- An empirical study—This kind of evaluation is rarely possible in real-world settings. This method assumes that it is possible to select two groups (either randomly or by matching each subject in the two groups by gender, educational background, and/or other socioeconomic factors) and to provide the treatment (that is the program of services) to one group but not to the other. Under these conditions, some test or inventory that measures what the experimental group was supposed to learn or accomplish is administered to both groups. It is expected that the scores on this test or inventory will be significantly higher for the experimental group (those who received the services) than for the control group (those who did not receive the services).

Step 7. Determine the content of the program and the methods by which it will be delivered.

The objectives clearly define the outcomes that you want your clients to achieve. Now we need to determine what elements of content your program must include in order to produce those outcomes. Note the following objectives and the alternative methods for meeting them.

Objective 1. "… state their interests as a description of a Holland code."

Methods for accomplishing:

a. use the Holland Party Game

b. administer the Self-Directed Search

c. use the Holland Career Game at the University of Missouri website (see Online Web Resources for web address)

Objective 2. "… describe and demonstrate that they can use at least three methods of identifying openings for the jobs in which they are interested."

Methods for accomplishing:

a. teach clients how to conduct informational interviews

b. teach clients how to use websites that list job postings

c. assist clients to build a social network using LinkedIn

Objective 3. "… prepare a job application or resume that highlights their skills for a particular job."

Methods for accomplishing:

a. hold a workshop on job applications and resumes

b. have clients use software that is loaded on computers in the career center

c. teach clients to use a website that offers templates for different types of resumes and job applications

At this point in the process someone on the development team may find it helpful to complete a form like the one shown in Figure 1.3. You may need to search through the catalogues or websites of major publishers of career planning materials to identify resources developed for the age group, reading level, and objectives of your target population. You may be able to identify multiple products that can contribute to two or more objectives. Then you will have an opportunity to compare the quality and cost of competitive products for use in your setting.

Your team may be unable to find existing products for some content areas. In that case, some activities or materials will have to be developed to support or to bridge between content units. It is likely, for example, that material to support objective 4 under the first need in Figure 1.3 ("… will be able to, in a mock interview, relate personal skills and experience to the job in each company") would have to be developed. Depending upon the nature of the objective and the expertise available on your staff, you may be able to develop these materials on site or contract this task out to a consultant or an organization.

Besides identifying content and resources, it is also necessary in this phase to decide upon the methods for delivering the content. These may include any of the following:

• One-on-one, face-to-face delivery by a career services provider—This is, of course, the most expensive approach both in dollars and time. Thus, it should be reserved for those individuals and/or for those units of content that need it most.

• Group face-to-face delivery by a counselor or facilitator—In this mode, a group leader presents material or leads activities. This could include group instruction and interaction about how to identify job openings and how to develop the documents (e.g., resume and cover letter) needed for a successful job search. Another example is group administration of an interest inventory and interpretation of its meaning. Obviously, this is a far less expensive way to deliver service since the cost of the leader's time can be divided by the number of persons in the group to calculate a per-hour cost of service.

Figure 1.3
Planning Sheet for Program Development

Need 1. Clients need to know how to find a job.

Possible objectives: After clients receive services from our center, they will be able to

1. List three specific jobs for which they are qualified

2. List three local companies that offer such jobs

3. Describe each company and how the job is performed there

4. In a mock interview, relate personal skills and experience to each job

5. Fill out a sample job application neatly and completely

Possible services or products to meet needs:

- Perform formal or informal assessment to identify skills and related occupations.

- Use a local website to identify companies and information about them.

- Teach clients how to schedule and conduct an informational interview.

- Ask someone from the human resources department of a local company to hold mock interviews with clients after the clients have attended a one-hour interview training session.

- Videotape mock interviews and give clients feedback.

- Acquire job application forms from a local company, have clients practice completing them, and provide feedback.

Possible ways to determine if the objectives have been met:

At the end of the sequence of activities ask clients to complete a questionnaire that asks for information related to the first three objectives. Evaluate objective 4 from a review of the videotapes; evaluate the success of objective 5 from a review of the completed job application forms.

(continued on next page)

Figure 1.3, continued

Need 2. Clients need to know how to change from one job to another

Possible objectives: After clients receive services from our center, they will be able to

1. List at least two jobs they would like

2. Describe the usual work tasks, skills, training required, employment outlook, and salary range for each job

3. Complete an action plan form that includes how and when they will complete the needed education or training

4. Describe how they will manage finances and other concerns (child care, transportation, access to the Internet for course work, etc.)

Possible services or products to meet needs:

- Use assessment inventories or informal techniques to identify transferable skills.

- Use Internet websites for job searching.

- Use print materials and websites for acquiring data about occupations.

- Complete a personal action plan, complete with long-range goals, short-range goals, and target dates for accomplishing each.

- Use websites to find ways to get training.

- Help clients find possible sources for funding of training.

- Delivery via software or websites—An ever-increasing array of software is available for use on stand-alone workstations or on the web. This software ranges from stand-alone pieces (such as an online version of an interest inventory or of the *Occupational Outlook Handbook*) to comprehensive web-based career planning systems. Similarly, websites that offer career information or career planning activities are growing at a phenomenal rate. Clients can use such tools in a library, at home, on a smart phone, or in a computer lab where many clients can work at the same time. This mode of delivery is low cost and effective when surrounded by human support.

- A virtual career center—A virtual career center is a well-planned website that creates a master menu of existing no-fee sites that offer component pieces of an integrated career-planning system. For example, one site may offer an interest inventory that yields a Holland code; a second site might allow a search for occupations and postsecondary majors by Holland code;

a third site might offer a postsecondary school search; while a fourth site offers excellent instruction and tools for the job search. Thus, someone who understands the elements of an integrated career-planning system may assemble a list of well-developed sites and put them all together under one menu that offers many or most of these components. In doing so, using a Google search to find such sites may be very helpful. Using the screened list maintained by Margaret Riley Dikel and displayed on the website of the National Career Development Association would be an even better way to identify sites for use in a virtual career center. The following sites are representative of the topics and appearance of virtual career centers: the University of Maryland Career Center, the Department of Labor's Career OneStop, and the Department of Labor's MyNextMove (see Online Web Resources for web addresses of each of these sites).

- Self-help print and audiovisual materials—Career centers typically contain a large number of self-help materials including books, videos, and audio tapes. Many clients benefit from using these materials on their own when they use them as an integrated part of the career planning or job search process.

Programs of service typically combine two or more of these methods of content delivery. How they are blended together depends upon the resources available. The overarching goal is to effectively meet the needs of as many clients as possible at the lowest per-client cost. The outcome of this phase should be a document that details the program(s) of service to be delivered. It should include the measurable objectives, the content and materials to accomplish these, the time to be devoted to the various units of the content, and the methods to be used to deliver it.

Step 8. Determine needed resources.

This step involves reviewing the resources needed and available for use in the delivery of the program or services. *Resources* can be defined as anything you need to further develop, deliver, and evaluate the program or services that you have described. Thus, resources may include administrative support; time of staff members and clients; use of facilities, hardware, web connectivity, software, and materials; and expertise that can be assigned to the development and delivery of the program. Unfortunately, most career programs have to do much with little funding, regardless of the setting. For this reason many programmatic decisions are not theory or practice based, but budget based. By this time in the development process, you have a clear picture of the needs of your clients and what your organization has to offer to meet these needs. So, your resources can be viewed in three categories: (a) those you already have, (b) those that you have the budget to purchase, and (c) those that you may be able to borrow or have to do without. In identifying this last category, it will be helpful to look at your list of stakeholders and what they may be able to provide.

During this step of the process, some of the following questions may prove helpful:

- Should a part-time or full-time employee be added?

- Should a consultant be hired to assist with program design?

- Should another computer be requested?

- Should software be licensed?

- Should tests, books, or videos be purchased?

- Should an Internet connection be established?

You may be asked to express your opinion on some of these matters, to review different products and recommend which to acquire, or to identify publishers and find out the cost of specific materials. The end product of this step will be the listing of all needed resources, when and where they will be acquired, and who has the responsibility to do so. This step may also include the preparation of a budget for obtaining needed staff and other resources.

Step 9. Identify significant barriers.

It is rare that any endeavor is implemented without barriers. You will be able to identify possible barriers by reviewing Step 1 (Environmental Scan), Step 4 (Stakeholders), and Step 8 (Resources). When you review your environment, you may find differences in the goals of your program and those of others who have influence in your environment. Among your stakeholders, you may find one or more who is jealous of your ability to offer the program or who has a stake in seeing it fail. Reviewing the list of needed resources, you may find that there is insufficient budget to acquire the staff or materials that you need or insufficient time on the part of needed personnel to develop and deliver the program. Other barriers may include lack of buy-in from your management, a poor marketing plan, an insufficient number of participants, or some change in local or governmental policies that affect the planning that has already taken place. The end product of this phase will be a list of possible or anticipated barriers and a back-up plan to manage each barrier if it presents itself.

Step 10. Develop a plan for promotion and marketing.

The proposed program, still on paper, must be promoted to at least three audiences: those who will receive it, those who will support it administratively, and stakeholders, especially those needed to contribute resources. Other audiences may include the community, mid-level managers, funding sources, parents, etc., depending on the setting.

There are two types of promotion: external and internal. External promotion is the marketing of your program to those who will receive it and to external stakeholders. Internal promotion is marketing of your program to internal stakeholders. Those who will receive the program may or may not be highly motivated to receive it. Obviously, the less motivated they are, the more promotion the program will need.

When planning external promotion, it is important to ask yourself a series of questions such as the following:

- Who is the target audience?

- Where is the target audience located?

- What sources of information are they most likely to pay attention to?

- Which media outlets will be best to reach your audience?

These methods may include the Internet (website, e-mail, social networking), billboards and signs, word of mouth, press releases, printed materials (brochures, letters, newsletters), and dissemination of information in collaboration with stakeholders.

Internal promotion is equally important in assuring that your program is a success. A first step is to identify any concerns that the stakeholders for the program may have. A second step is to determine how to help them understand the need for the program. Using an advisory committee that represents the key groups (such as WIA Boards, the funding agency, community, employers, management, clients) can be helpful in gaining buy-in for the program. It is important to invite people to this group who have the visibility and power to help you promote the program.

For some, the presentation of data or research findings will gain support. The stakeholders and advisory committee need to be constantly informed about the needs of the target population, the objectives and content of your program, and its expected effectiveness. Such reports can be given via person-to-person communication, through print reports provided at periodic intervals, via a website, or through informal word-of-mouth feedback from those who have profited from the program.

If the program has been offered previously, an important piece of internal (and, in some cases, external) promotion is providing data about how many people have used the services or programs and how they have evaluated them. You can add a personal touch by telling the story of specific cases that demonstrate the kinds of results desired. Sharing the results of questionnaires completed by clients can be useful. Using these kinds of tools will help you to persuasively communicate client satisfaction, achievement, and outcomes.

Another method that can be used for positive public relations is called the A > R > B formula (Hoppin & Splete, 1996). Program *activities* (A) bring about *results* (R), which are measured through observation, client satisfaction questionnaires, and exit interviews. These results translate to *benefits* (B). These benefits accrue to the people you serve, your organization and, potentially, society in general. For example, a successful program of services that assists 80% of its clients (needing to find a job and keep it for at least a year) reaps these kinds of benefits:

For the individuals:

- Increased life satisfaction and enhanced lifestyle
- Improved self-concept and sense of personal responsibility
- Ability to support themselves and their families

For your organization:

- Capability to meet goals set by management and/or funding sources
- Increased motivation of employees to succeed
- Personal satisfaction of career services providers and other helpers

For society:

- Less need to spend tax dollars to support individuals
- Larger tax base
- Potential for reduced crime, substance abuse, and family violence

Remember, external and internal promotion are extremely important both because people need the services and because success must be achieved in order to keep the support of management. Failure to attend to promotion may result in loss of funding and psychological support for your valuable services.

Step 11. Deliver the program.

If all of the previous steps have been completed, this stage of the development process should be easy. Those who deliver the program will have the needed budget, staff, materials, and other resources. The objectives, time frame, and content will be clear. The end product of this step will be a very detailed plan for delivery of your program which includes tasks, timelines, and responsibility for items such as the following:

- Acquiring administrative approval for delivering the program

- Securing budget, if needed

- Determining the length, frequency, and specific dates of offering the program

- Developing or acquiring the curriculum to be taught

- Determining whether delivery will be face to face or online

- Selecting instructors/facilitators

- Purchasing equipment, assessments, and/or other resources

- If online, uploading instructional materials and creating online discussion forums

- If face to face, acquiring facilities and equipment for the training

- Developing brochures, articles, e-mails, and other methods of promotion

- Promoting the program

- Selecting, inviting, and registering participants

- Duplicating materials

- Making visuals if needed

- Planning all details (parking, meals and/or breaks, etc.) related to the day and time of program delivery

- Developing or acquiring materials related to evaluation

- Preparing a summary report and providing feedback to stakeholders

It is helpful to categorize tasks into major and subtasks along with the assignment of responsibility for the task and a date for completion.

Step 12. Revise the program based on the experience of delivering it and evaluating it.

Programs seldom reach perfection, especially not at the first or second pass. So, at this step of the development process your team will use the experience of delivering the program and the results of the evaluation to define specific ways that it can be improved next time. Based on this initial experience, you may decide to revise your objectives, change your methods or materials for delivering content, or alter your methods of evaluation. You may also choose to change or expand your methods of promotion.

It is very important to capture these revision ideas in writing immediately after delivery of the program. The team involved in program development and delivery should meet and openly discuss the strengths and weaknesses of the program. They should also brainstorm ideas about how to make changes next time.

Supportive Roles

Though you, as a facilitator, may be involved throughout this development process, there are some very specific tasks that you will almost surely be asked to assume: case management, instruction, group facilitation, and/or involvement in the career center. Let's consider each of these specific tasks separately.

The first supportive role is case management. The clients you serve need to be viewed as individuals with unique needs even though they may be treated at times as members of a group. You are likely to write down the specific services the client needs as well as barriers that may exist. Needs may include attendance at specific group sessions, use of resources in the career center, and services offered on a one-on-one basis. Further, dealing with the needs or barriers may include referral to other agencies, getting additional training, or receiving support services such as childcare or transportation.

Case management is the process of assuring that these services are offered to the client, that sufficient information is provided about ways to take advantage of the services, and that there is follow-through after termination. You may have this responsibility, or a counselor or supervisor may have it. You may be keeping notes in the client's folder or computer record about how the client was served, the result of each intervention, the client's progress in working through an action plan, and next steps that should be taken. Thus, case management is a process of monitoring the client from the intake interview through termination and follow-through related to the action plan that is developed for each individual client. If client records, action plans, and weekly activities are all entered into a database that links these components, it would be possible to receive weekly reports that provide the data needed for systematic case management. Although instruction, group facilitation, and interviewing require strong "people skills", case management requires strong organizational skills.

A second strong support role is *instruction*. This role involves teaching the client specific knowledge, skills, or behaviors needed to succeed in accomplishing career goals. This instruction would ideally be given to groups of clients in order to reduce the time and money spent. Common topics of instruction include how to research occupations or jobs, use the Internet, identify job openings, write a resume, build an e-portfolio, and participate in a job interview. Attendance and participation in such training should be included in client action plans and monitored through case management.

Although the word *instruction* implies that the career services provider may deliver content to a group of people, often in a lecture format, the word *facilitation*, a third likely task, implies that a practitioner will assist or motivate clients to participate in and complete group or online activities. Examples of group facilitation include leading informal assessment activities (such as the Holland Party Game), group administration of tests or inventories, helping a group to explore a specific website, or leading a group in identifying their skills.

A fourth supporting task may be the ongoing review of websites that will support the delivery of services. These sites may be organized as a virtual career center. It is also totally feasible to provide interactive assistance to clients through e-mail, audio conferencing, video conferencing, and chat capabilities. As this trend grows, career services providers may do some of their work with individuals and/or groups via the Internet.

Summary

Career services providers have a wide range of responsibilities related to program planning and implementation. Their roles include active participation in the systematic process of program development, individual case management, instruction, group facilitation, and ongoing review of career-related websites that can be used in stand-alone mode or in an organized virtual career center. This unit focuses on a detailed 12-step process for program development, and offers the opportunity to apply that process to a program that can be delivered at your work site.

ACTIVITY #2:
Select a specific target population that you now work with or hope to work with. Then think about their needs related to career development or job placement. Build a program to address one or more of those needs. If possible, develop a program that you will be able to use after completion of this course.

Program Planning Worksheet

Group Name: _____

Date: _____

Members of Group: _____

Group Leader: _____

Group Recorder: _____

Instructions: Select a specific target population that you now work with or hope to work with. Then think about their needs related to career development or job placement. Build a program to address one or more of those needs. If possible, develop a program that you will be able to use after completion of this course.

Step 1: Environmental Scan – List at least five (5) characteristics of the environment in which this program will be launched—such as amount of support from management or availability of funding. Complete the following sentence in at least five different ways.

In the environment for our program,

1. _____

2. _____

3. _____

4. _____

5. _____

Step 2: Target Population – List at least five (5) characteristics of the population you wish to serve with the program you are developing. Complete the following sentence in at least five different ways.

People who will participate in this program...

1. _____

2. _____

3. _____

4. _____

5. _____

Step 3: Needs – List at least five (5) needs that you believe this population has by completing the following sentence.

People who are expected to attend this program need...

1. _____

2. _____

3. _____

4. _____

5. _____

By which method(s) will you clarify or specify these needs?

_____

Step 4: Stakeholders – Identify at least five (5) stakeholders in your program, and indicate whether each is internal (I) to your organization or external (E).

The primary stakeholders for our program are

                                                     (Circle one.)

1. _____   I   E

2. _____   I   E

3. _____   I   E

4. _____   I   E

5. _____   I   E

Step 5: Measurable Objectives – Write 3-5 concrete, measurable objectives for your program by completing the following sentence.

At the end of this program, participants will be able to

1. _____

2. _____

3. _____

4. _____

5. _____

Program Planning Worksheet, continued

Step 6: Evaluation – For each of the objectives listed in Step 5, and in the same order, indicate the method(s) you will use to measure its accomplishment.

1. _____

2. _____

3. _____

4. _____

5. _____

Step 7: Program Content and Delivery – Provide an outline of the content you plan to deliver, and in the spaces provided on the right, indicate how (face-to-face instruction, website, video, assessment, etc.) each component will be delivered.

I. _____

    a. _____ _____

    b. _____ _____

    c. _____ _____

II. _____

    a. _____ _____

    b. _____ _____

    c. _____ _____

III. _____

    a. _____ _____

    b. _____ _____

    c. _____ _____

IV. _____

    a. _____ _____

    b. _____ _____

    c. _____ _____

(**Note:** If more space is needed, continue on another sheet of paper.)

Step 8: Resources – Make a list of all of the items you will need in order to deliver your program. In the spaces on the right, indicate that you already have it, will purchase it, or will borrow it.

1._____   _____

2._____   _____

3._____   _____

4._____   _____

5._____   _____

6._____   _____

7._____   _____

8._____   _____

Step 9: Barriers – In the spaces below, list up to 5 barriers or problems that may arise as you plan and implement your program. In the spaces on the right of each barrier, indicate at least one possible way to overcome this barrier.

1._____   _____

2._____   _____

3._____   _____

4._____   _____

5._____   _____

Program Planning Worksheet, continued

Step 10: Marketing and Promotion – List and explain 3-5 ways in which you will advertise and market your program both internally and externally.

1. _____

Explain: _____

2. _____

Explain: _____

3. _____

Explain: _____

4. _____

Explain: _____

5. _____

Explain: _____

Notes you would like to add:

References

Hoppin, J., & Splete, H. (Eds). (1996). *Curriculum for career development facilitators.* Rochester: MI: Oakland University.

Kirkpatrick, D. L. (1994). *Evaluating training programs.* San Francisco: Berrett-Koehler Publishers, Inc.

Super, D. E. (1988). *Adult Career Concerns Inventory.* Vocopher. (See Online Web Resources for web address).

Resources

Edds, C. (2008). *How to market career development programs and services.* Broken Arrow, OK: National Career Development Association.

Elsdon, R. (2010). *Building workforce strength: Creating value through workforce and career development.* Santa Barbara, CA: Ron Elsdon, editor.

Gysbers, N., & Henderson, P. (2005). *Comprehensive guidance programs that work.* Austin, TX: Pro-Ed.

Osborn, D., Riley Dikel, M., & Sampson, J. P., Jr. (2011). *The Internet: A tool for career planning* (3rd ed.). Broken Arrow, OK: National Career Development Association.

Whitfield, E. A., Feller, R. W., & Wood, C. (2008). *A counselor's guide to career assessment* (5th ed.). Broken Arrow, OK: National Career Development Association.

Kirkpatrick, D. L. (1994). *Evaluating training programs.* San Francisco: Berrett-Koehler Publishers, Inc.

Sampson, J. P., Jr. (2008). *Designing and implementing career programs: A handbook for effective practice.* Broken Arrow, OK: National Career Development Association.

Schutt, D. (2007). *How to plan and develop a career center.* (2nd ed.) Chicago, IL: Ferguson Publishing Company.

Online Web Resources

The following is a list of online references and resources recommended for this unit. By the very nature of the Internet, this list cannot be inclusive of all available resources. As such, NCDA invites recommendations from participants on references and resources.

This list will be updated on NCDA's website (http://www.ncda.org) periodically. Additionally, the use of *The Internet: A tool for career planning, third edition* (available from NCDA) is recommended. A list of updated links from this book is also maintained on NCDA's website.

Note: The National Career Development Association and the authors and editors of this list of resources make no claim as to the accuracy and validity of the information presented on the websites below. The content of the sites below are the property of their respective owners and editors. No warranty, either express or implied, is made by the inclusion of a website on this list.

National Career Development Guidelines — http://associationdatabase.com/aws/NCDA/asset_manager/get_file/3384/ncdguidelines2007.pdf

Internet Sites for Career Planning — http://associationdatabase.com/aws/NCDA/pt/sp/resources

University of Maryland Career Center — http://www.careercenter.umd.edu/

CareerOneStop — http://www.careeronestop.org/

My Next Move — http://www.mynextmove.org/

Vocopher — http://www.vocopher.com

If you found this Career Knowledge Series information helpful, you may be interested in learning more about NCDA's Career Development Facilitator program. This program makes practical Career Development training available to individuals in a variety of settings and also prepares individuals for a valuable professional credential. For more information, check out **www.ncda.org**